STAN THE MAN
BACK TO BASICS

Bruce Piasecki

 ISBN: 979-8-31780-399-5 hard cover

TABLE OF CONTENTS

JOYFUL PROSE: AN INTRODUCTION, BY MIA FUNK

Founder of the Creative Process podcast series. (This Creative Process series is a production shared widely for free on Tune In, Google, YouTube, Spotify, and over one hundred of today's universities globally.)

The writing style of this fable is a rich, introspective blend of realism and surrealism, characterized by its use of vivid, sensory details and dreamlike sequences. The narrative flows between the protagonist Stan's everyday life and his inner world, often blurring the lines between reality, memory, and imagination. This style creates a layered, contemplative atmosphere that invites readers to engage deeply with the themes of the story.

We have seen this before in Proust, Joyce, and their descendants, but in the hands of Piasecki there is before us in each page the weight of the real world and its torrent of problems. Bruce Piasecki, as the author of a dozen books of non-fiction and a set of biographies, is well prepared to pursue this parable close to the issues of our time, a fable fabulous in its dreams but practical in its rich texture.

The prose is marked by a lyrical quality, especially in its descriptions of Stan's thoughts and dreams. The narrative often shifts in tone and structure, moving from straightforward depictions of Stan's daily routines to more poetic, almost stream-of-consciousness passages during his dreams. These shifts can be disorienting but also serve to mirror the complexities of human consciousness, where past, present, and future frequently intermingle.

The style's effect on the reader is multifaceted. On one hand, it encourages a reflective reading experience, prompting readers to consider their own lives, relationships, and the passage of time. The frequent references to faith, tradition, and mortality may evoke a sense of nostalgia or introspection. Many of these beliefs are seen embedded in imaginative and insightful passages that challenge readers to piece together the story's deeper meanings, making the act of reading this short parable an active, engaging process.

Overall, the writing style enhances the fable's messages about the importance of family, faith, and the search for meaning in the face of life's inevitable changes. It conveys the idea that life is a complex, interconnected journey, where the mundane and the profound are inseparable. The narrative's poetic and reflective qualities help to underscore the themes of mortality, legacy, and the enduring significance of human connection, leaving the reader with a sense of both the fragility and the beauty of life.

All of Piasecki's books explore the tensions between the past, the present, and our near future. He asks in new ways "What is enough?" and "What is joy in this new swift and severe world?"

From his Cornell dissertation on Walt Whitman and the American Estimate of Nature, to his *New York Times* bestseller *Doing More with Less* about Ben Franklin and his contemporary big lessons of the past with the emerging near future before us. He does this with humor, poise, and astute generosity. Come to this parable for some fanciful and fundamental answers.

While this book before you is Bruce's most dramatically creative, the pattern of his corpus is clear and aligned. Bruce feels we can do better and must by returning to the civic lessons humanity has learnt and felt before. Many of these beliefs are embedded in the clever dreams and day-to-day activities of the lead character in *Stan the Man*, a Long Island high school janitor. Leave it to Bruce to see this world in the actions of this man Stan.

This book offers bursts of creative social history with humanitarian grandeur, and remains a profound celebration of the creative force of everyday people. Welcome into this sparkling world of Bruce Piasecki's prose and narrative skill.

FIRST SEQUENCE: STEPPING INTO HISTORY

Stan the man is more than his job.

Stan is a janitor at the Beach Street High School, not far from the strong waves of Robert Moses State Beach. On weekends, he cleans a series of mansions in Magoon Landing, a region across the water, work that Stan calls "wealth gigs.".

Stan works these extra locations to "make ends meet," as he says, and his family lives a good life thanks to Stan. Some of his kids play sax, some kids play around, some take military schooling seriously. He supports a big family.

Some of the teenage kids at his day job, still happy from their weekends at the beach, each Monday morning bring sand in their socks and shoes. Yet Stan does not make a big thing out of it; he has learned through time, since leaving Poland, to be mostly invisible at his jobs. Invisible, but steadfast. His dress and accent kept its Polish continental flair.

Stan is a brilliant man, self-informing and curious. Stan is a modern man, a warm man. He, being near retirement age, survived a good part of the last century. He never made it to serve, like friends, in the Pacific or Korea or Vietnam, since Stan has horrible eyesight. But his hearing is exceptional and alert, and his memory is at times prying and intimidating. This makes Stan a supportive conversationalist with all ages, the rich and the poor.

Stan might seem both old school and old world, yet there is new-world attitude in his walk. In his Converse black sneakers, he is both a throw-back yet remarkably contemporary. Sparkling janitorial keys fling from his hips, and because of the swing, many of the girls at school like him.

Stan knows a daughter of President Obama as “a young buddy” in the hallways he cleans. He even knows several articulate media legends and TV personalities from his extra weekend jobs. They are often surprised how up on the news Stan the man is. What they do not see is that Stan he has a bug in his ear for the news all workday, as he sweeps and washes.

He is friendly, and at most times warm. Unlike the teachers that hound them relentlessly for their rebellious behaviors, the kids are fond of Stan. They often find him playing his accordion by the playground at lunch break, those keys swinging from his hips as he plays.

But before we begin, a warning: this tale knows that no matter how much you are liked, nor how many of the rich and powerful you know, you are still you, and alone in your dreams.

Stan the Navigator

It is 1145 AD, many years before the discovery of America. A precise date often starts a Stan dream. Stan, when in the past, can prove the navigator of his dreams, a dream-type he loves for its expansiveness and wild roaming. In this case, he flies fast and furious.

In Stan's 1145 dream (the last time he saw on his night clock that night) he recalls how the chronicler Otto von Freising met in Italy a well-dressed Syrian bishop, with pearls and exotic silk. The Syrian, like in a movie, spoke in English, not Italian.

This short dream meeting created an actual legal charter, and a popular hoax, where Stan swept it, the letter crispy to his touch, up in a barrel. The original letter was also, strangely, in English.

This hoax letter recounted in specific terms and colors and glories the opulence of the Prester's realm. Prester John was a smallish man compared to the Syrian, but he was a great talker. And the tale began like a long-tallish history by Walter Isaacson, Robert Caro, or Taylor Branch, abstract names Stan saw in the school library. While Stan was not there, except in this dream, he was the navigator, not the historian pretending he was there.

The discovered letter told those ready to be fooled how Prester's wealth and power exceeded that of all the known monarchs of the world. The Syrian, Stan, and even Prester John himself could not convey in the dream its immensity, as we know it can be with the dreams that seem deep and dark and endless.

You could not do a flyover of the realm. Prester's domain had to be imagined by the European, and by Stan, as it roamed into three distinct Indias and extended across the deserts of Babylon to include the Tower of Babel. Asia to Africa, to the smaller Americas, Antarctica and then Europe, these were smallish areas, failed continents, compared to the taller tales of the man himself. Stan felt glorious.

Stan is now back home, in his pajamas, and it is no longer 1145. Morning again.

It feels more like time to watch sports highlights this morning, where he can put a microscope on the key plays of the day before without effort. In last night's dreamwork, Stan felt it took him at least four months of horse travel to span the imaginary lord's lands. He was ready for ordinary time,

His wife smiled "Good morning, Vietnam." She liked to joke about peace, about peace in America, built by the many for the few.

If you read the history books, the actual navigator, Henry, found new worlds that helped the Portuguese get up the gusto to explore beyond the norms of their day and century. Part of the gusto was listening to the tall tales of Henry the Navigator chirping about realms owned by Prester. Our unassuming hero Stan overheard from the high school science teacher the day before an ear full about the ancient Portuguese navigator, who took the risks at sea and land, changed Europe and the world.

Those overheard school talks became the enabling fragments that started Stan's navigator dreams in the first place.

But how did a simple man like Stan know all the rest? By vivid dreaming. Stan simply stepped back into history with a few friends at night, in dream.

This routine helped Stan believe his life well worth living; and he became aware that his beliefs from these dreams made his days richer than any could imagine.

Turtles and Titles

The turtle of love and joy floats, with big happy eyes, near Stan on his lucky nights. Bubbles of happiness ascend from her, with questions in each bubble.

Something about a turtle makes Stan the man stand taller. We feel this when we stand near everyday friends, but Stan made it magical with his night friend, the turtle.

Whenever Stan is having a fine youthful dream, the turtle swims near him like a moving religious icon. She opens the door to the ocean of longing in Stan, a door built not in wood but in his imagination, with hinges made for treasure and children and everlasting peace.

The turtle has a title, something royal and supreme, but not published like a book title. In her secret and silent smile, she journeys forth, floating and famous without the need for publicity. She floats past the mechanical everyday realm of Stan's workaday world. By staying near her in his dreams, Stan leaves the world of stoves and screws, nails and sharp nothings, that divide us by race and riches.

On the surface of Stan's days, the sun bakes the land into a grey mass of cars and creatures and malls and stores, as if the cyclone meant for Oz is nearing Long Island. But at night, it all changes again. The turtle reappears, sparkling with joy and curiosities, beyond the surface whirling. There is a new literacy in Stan's life when the turtle reads the waves each night, and they proceed.

The surrounding ocean of each dream does not bind him in girdles but instead in giggles. She is his wonderful wizard of warmth, full of snickers. She is about gurgles not babbles. He finds her a gargle, a mouthwash, and rinse of his sillier adult self. As when near her, he is all titters and not sniggers. She can fondle the playfulness near him without worry—and does so furiously.

Turtles, to kids and their parents, are both old-world and new-world like Stan. They have ancient protections in their shells, like his proven faith. Yet turtle arms swim and walk forward into a future like kid's play. They are not armed with troubles, and like Stan, they do not meddle with things beyond their grasp.

Yertle the Turtle, the famous turtle of Seussian lore, was terrible in the way he stacked his tale with ambition and height, until he fell. Stan's turtle remains nameless, and sweet, famous only in his dreams.

The Beach Street Gymnasium

The high school gym is a massive place, like a king's throne in the school. It houses high hoops for the ambitious, and an abundance of stands to watch the competitive. Combined all together, many of the teaching rooms could fit inside the gymnasium. So Stan starts sweeping there most mornings when fresh.

Stan likes the swirls of dust under the stands best, swirls magnetized to themselves, like puffs of hair hitting a barber's floor.

Many of the boys, and three of the girls (Alice, Nina, and Lily) played stick ball outside the gym by the time he got there. Stick ball and wiffle ball, with plenty of wiffle balls to play toss in the wind with the girls and boys.

It is a brisk and beautiful Long Island morning. Being with the girls in the gym makes Stan feel timeless, young again. This stick ball game starts minutes before school, is short and explosive, as the days in May are already long. Stan cleans the gym, as they play. Stan hears their music, which becomes part of his music-based dreams many nights. Time now for school itself.

It is probable that until the middle of the 1300s no European travelled east of Baghdad, the high school history teacher noted as Stan swept. He paused as he realized an important turning point in human history. You did not meet a wall stopping the Europeans. Instead, you simply met silence, knowing neither language nor custom to proceed further unless a fool.

The Crusades had given some human knowledge of Syria, Palestine, and some parts of Asia Minor. Yet much farther down the road, most of the Orient remained cut off. Sweeping the gym that day let Stan prepare for a wiffle ball game in his next dream, and a flight to the 1300s.

Actuality on Long Island and at Sea

Alice, Nina, and Lily. A trinity of sorts, displaying youth and vigor and verve.

For some reason, probably kissing, two of the three wiffle ball girls got sick the next day. Stan's nose was a bit stuffy from cleaning beneath the gymnasium stands yesterday, but two of these three girls missed school for a few days, sick.

Stan cared for these girls, but he could not pay too much attention to their sore throats without notice, so he simply felt bad for them those days, both at work and in his dreams. He would give them candy when they were better.

In dreams based on their absence, the happy days leading up to further adventures were disrupted by the Black Death of 1348 to 1349. This development in the lectures made the medieval world shake at its stone-like foundations.

Stan started to look at some of the boys hovering near Lily like Ottoman Turks, strongmen that should be watched, and when they approached, appeased. This week he overheard that the descendants of Kublai Khan were driven out of the Chinese capital in 1368, but Stan's sense of geography was so poor that some of this seemed to him impossible, as he swept the head office that day. He wished he could ask for clarification during lunch from the girls.

The girl who did not get sick that wiffle ball game was the Italian one, a Jewish family from Venice. She cleared up Stan's head about why some of her ancestors were rumored to trade with the Orient, bringing jewels into her family in the Mediterranean.

Later he learned that her family had established a near-monopoly amounting to a stranglehold on Egyptian trade many moons before the family came to Long Island. All of this seemed too good to be true to Stan, but he liked talking to her about family and past fame.

The Adriatic, the Archipelago, and old Alexandria, these were within range of the young lady's wiffle-ball bat, her family memories a lifeline to the richness of their world. And Stan saw much more in the strength of her swing and her strong thighs. He saw in her thighs the future, as they ran the bases with grace and good will and superb timing. The boys tried unsuccessfully to throw them out around the bases.

Watching the girls run, superior lessons descended inside his skull to teach him. Always hit the base as you run past it. That is basic. Do not miss the turn. This was the fundamental joy in gaming, and perhaps in life, he felt. Take it one base at a time.

Travelling in dreams to all those places the kids and teachers spoke about make him think about the evolution of the nervous system, from the original nerve net to the flatworm. Stan remembers that the great writer Bill McKibben once said that corporation heads had "the intelligence of a flatworm." Wrong, he thought, being basic. For after the flatworm came the grains segmented into single nerve cords like the arthropod, and then we had fish and man. And then the spring in Lily and Grace. Each step, as they approached each base. It was wonderful to watch each morning.

As he travelled with time in his mighty night dreams, the full nervous system of humanity matured exactly like it was supposed to. Fallen humans failed to recognize this basic grandness of all types. While he had ambitions once to become a sex maniac, he failed the practicalities of this every day. Stan remained reserved and observant and happy and accepting and inclusive and happy.

Looking at Grace and Lily run from afar proved enough.

This basic richness was worth magnifying. Flying over his citizens' townships in his dreams, and even the largest banks he'd spy on from Manhattan trains, he felt he could quadruple his wealth by simply folding his bills in fourths. He kept his family in shape and happy by simply folding the maniac drives as well, unlike so many others on Long Island.

Imagining More Peaceful Decades

One of Stan's relatives became a Harvard-educated spinal and head-injury doctor.

How the hell did that happen?

It is America after all. Hell—it is America, land of science and land of the free. These robust accomplishments in Stan's family came about despite the wilds of prejudice they faced upon arrival.

From the limbic forebrain areas of her brain to that doctor's hypothalamus, to the midbrain, to his firm hindbrain, to the spinal cord and the ganglia, there are visceral tissues these kids use when they play wiffle ball, and there are visceral tissues Stan uses when he sweeps the gym. He loved how Grace ran to first base on a base hit. Without being near, he could use his dream strengths to feel her heart rate getting faster from afar.

Amazing stuff it is, to contemplate these visceral loops. But actuality never stopped Stan's imagination from wandering past actual history into the fabulous at sea.

His past was his history as the actual content of his life entered his dreams. After a fine dream, he often felt like a sweaty member of the Apollo 13 moon mission, where his fantastic tale of recovery and triumph shot back to Earth despite the fact that he never landed on the moon. If he wanted it bad enough, he could even navigate some of these dreams upon reentry to the ordinary atmosphere of his life.

All happy dreams resembled one another, he found, but each unhappy dream was unhappy in its own way.

Most of the time he was a happy child in a large Polish farm family whose menu consisted of one flash-like furious direction in a grand feeling of two choices: take it or leave it. He was wise enough to take it, whatever a dream sputtered and spouted forth.

From his view of the Earth from his dreams, he always wondered why the nations could not be more at peace in our blue spinning world, of ocean and borderless trust, of dolphins and astronauts.

The Maps Stan Stood Near

Standing by maps would often deliver Stan a superb evening dream.

This day a high school history teacher offered great slides projected on the wall. Stan stood near with these slides flashing before him, broom in hand. The lecture today was centered on the celebrated Catalan Atlas made in 1375 by Abraham Cresques, a Jew of Majorca, that portrayed the travels of Marco Polo, still celebrated by kids in pool time. Stan wondered if Nina, Lily, and Grace were descendants of these Jews.

While the history teacher never made it to the Bibliothèque Nationale in Paris to see the actual map, his slide of the map showed remarkable details.

Stan's near-photographic memory recorded what he saw for his nightwork. He could re-travel those dream paths while sweeping the floor or standing near the maps for a quick rest. His wrists wanted the rest, but his spirit wanted the travel in the maps. This, he felt, was the surround sound of ordinary life.

While Italy was full of the stories and poems and parables of Chaucer and Petrarch, somehow this map by Cresques showed that the Catalans knew how to imagine a larger world out there than the British or the Italians could. This thrilled Stan as he stood there, a deep listener when it concerned the past. His visual memory enhanced his dreams, as the residues of his days dusting were also the residues of his nights travelling.

Muscovy. Persia to the South. Arabia even farther south, then the spice smells of India and Turkestan to the East. Stan never left Long Island after leaving Poland and Newark. Yet the world was his oyster, as they say.

Different from the Americans who only cared about the price and distance to the local malls, Stan was the man, the modern man, in Converse sneakers.

He first recognized the genius in dreams on the day an unwanted dream destination had him in his mother's European tub with American toys that became, in the course of the dream, Thomas Edison's toaster and live radios. God gave him sufficient education in his longings without the need to become a killer.

Somehow, from the pieces of a few history talks overheard with the girls, he had pieced together enough to know the living links between medieval travel of the days of Marco Polo to the Renaissance voyages of the great Portuguese travelers about to set forth. Each dream trip sparkled like fireflies in his backyard.

He would come home that night, after a nap, and tell his kids what he had learned.

There were things of his day he would not mention to his kids. Her name is Lily, the older of the sick ones. Lily was the one well-off with rich ancestors. Her friend is named Grace. That much he knew. There is also a very confident Nina. These three became one turtle in some dreams.

He knew very little else of these wiffle-ball girls. Between them, he sensed that the one from Venice understood that her Italian ancestors had to have close ties to Persia to prosper. They were all very young, with great athletic legs. Speed never killed him in a dream of Lily or Grace, yet when they ended too suddenly, like when an athlete stops suddenly and you know them hurt, he would say: "I am not so think as you drunk I am."

He often would sit back the next afternoon after a Lily dream, and think he wished he had done so much more in his youth before marriage. But later he found out in his dreams that he had already done much.

One fact remained as centerpiece in his second dream: While those in power in Portugal committed to discovering the Cape route to India, they also were more widely roaming than the Italians. Somehow, he felt Lily more widely roaming in her life set forth at the high school than Grace, but he did not need to prove it.

Lily was seeking other places to find the wealth like the Portuguese of old.

In this way, Stan was like a kid from Long Island who knew enough about the city from the tales of those working or living in Manhattan, to be dangerous when talking about the city.

Be not afraid of life.

SECOND SEQUENCE: SKIPPING INTO YOUTH AND MUSIC

Cleaning Windows

His green truck refused to start this morning. That means two things have to happen: His music-loving older son has to wake up by noon to fix the truck; while Stan has to walk to work at Beach Street, not a short distance up Higbie Lane. Stan is prepared as usual, lunch in a box made by his wife, and his sneakers ready to "leave some leather."

He gets to work ten minutes early, time enough to watch Grace and Lily exchange a few compliments on their dress.

Like Marco Polo, Stan is lucky in life. Because he is so warm, and interesting, people share things with Stan, the things of their life, without him asking. They are interested in him, as Stan, as Stan the man, giving him each day more fragments for his dream work.

While much of the 15th century, and the early decades of the 16th, continued to be popular in search of pilgrimages to the Holy Land, Stan pays more attention to the history teacher's slides of the Portuguese travels. Why? He guesses that he is like those who got lost. He loves a sense of loss in travel, absolutely loves it.

Maybe to be more accurate, he feels the Portuguese were members of adventure, going forth with a turtle's confidence, and not seeking certainty before they started. Grace is more appealing to Stan since she is able to get lost in her fancies, and to be quite colorful as a young girl, while Lily is somewhat pre-determined in direction and temperament. Stan likes that most kids are not pre-determined.

That is why, after walking back from work that day, he was prepared to admire the lectures on Henry the Navigator, both for his adventures to African lands, and for his ability to create what the history teacher called "The House of Avis."

Most Americans felt that Avis meant a car rental club, but he knew better. From 1385 to 1580, the house of Avis roamed, and roamed like Stan's best dreams with his trusted turtle.

"Most Americans, what a dangerous phrase to assume," he thinks. Yet most Americans do respect folks like Henry David Thoreau, who stayed in Boston or Walden. Why respect dreamless folks that did not wander the globe of the unknown like our Portuguese Henry the Navigator? Stan cuts off this treacherous thought path.

Most Americans do know that Marco Polo was an adventurous Italian. Yet few know or have a clue who the House of Avis might be. This makes Stan reflect on his earlier self. He had always wanted to make up stories of how he and his wife got lost early in their relationships, since there was such a great velocity and variety to their actual travel then and in her night emotions. But being Polish and a janitor, he'd rather now simply walk to work.

The Game of Wiffle Ball

Even though his green truck got fixed by his son, it sounds like a rumble came to town. The girls playing wiffle ball with the many boys stop and yell "HELLO Stan." He likes that very much—their strong Long Island accents—like being called out in a game before thousands. Grace, although just over 16, is a smart, travelled kid, she often speaks of "emotional intelligence." She must have seen her mother carrying around the book.

One day, before school began, and the wiffle balls were almost still, he asked: "HEY HELLO GRACE." Grace, like a statue made of milk, stood dead still for a second, before she began to pour, not expecting a word from the janitor that had watched most of the morning season in silence. She said, nervously, "YES SIR?" He asked, "Tell me again, what is emotional intelligence?" The sounds of wiffle balls whizzed by.

She said emotional intelligence is "What you have, Stan. IQ is only 20 percent of success, my Mom says, and it is in a book, a good book from someone whose name combined Gold and Man.

"My Mom says you need persistence," she continued, "and the ability to motivate teams, and things like that."

He said: "COOL."

Her comment was received by others as well as high praise of Stan. It made his week, this new attention from the kids at work.

He could not stop himself: "Is that why you are so calm when you strike out? While the other kids get red in the face?"

She did not answer.

Emotional intelligence in the game of wiffle ball is beyond words. Reason and science may prefer the flights of straight lines, so they can make and erect exact signs. But Stan knew this basic truth above all else: the engines of emotion jump around, like a turtle in currents. Or perhaps more like a butterfly in the spring winds. They never walk a straight line. He was ok with this high fact.

Like a turtle that can advance from sea to shore, words remain secondary to adventure.

Music is Magical

He has broken the ice. The awkward silences were receding. He has gone from having the hobble of a turtle out of water to a father before youth. They now speak more frequently to him, viewing him as a trustworthy adult friend.

By mentioning strike outs, and then asking questions directly of Grace, basic shifts have happened in their exchange. He has heard them singing Van Morrison's "Brown Eyed Girl" once or twice before. He now wonders, footloose, that maybe they will talk more music with him the next morning.

> He starts to hum:
> "Oh, the smell of the bakery from across the street
> Got in my nose
> As we carried our ladders down the street
> With the wrought-iron gate rows.
> I went home and listened to Jimmi Rodgers in my lunch break,
> Bought five Woodbine at the shop on the corner
> And went straight back to work.
> What is my life?
> I'm happy cleaning windows
> Take my time, I'll see you when my love grows.
> Baby, don't let it slide, I'm a working man in my prime.
> Cleaning windows."

Stan, not being afraid of solitude, adds his basic gratitude to the joy behind this popular song—and the kids feel that joy. He has crossed a threshold again. It was as if Stan began saying what they wanted in life. The kids knew that most adults had in their selected scripts and catechisms a way to bottom out in vulnerabilities. Instead, this song gives them hope both in Stan and in their own lives, and a sense of adventure that helped them stand tall.

Stan's older son played bass to that Van Morrison set of songs several times in his basement the week before, so Stan the man could recall both cadence and the sweet pace of Van the man's words.

It struck both Grace, and Lily, and the dozen boys as "superb, Stan, superb."

Like an apostles' creed, the song was a protest song of youthful independence. It sang true to them playing wiffle ball that day, even if they, and Stan, had no clue what "five Woodbine" might be, and why "he went straight back to work."

This made Stan's month. It was like the time he found for free a bison leather front-pocket wallet in a student locker, one that fits as many cards as he owns. And his boss let Stan keep it, knowing the kid had moved closer to the city.

It is still only May. The smell of the flowering abundance is all around outside. The discovery of covering more ground with the kids by bringing up music offers new life to his appeal. It was as if he also has found a manicure set, and that others groomed him for better, more social conversations than a janitor normally qualifies for.

He had several weeks of service, cleaning windows and floors, before they all went home for the summer. He would miss Grace and Lily, in particular. Neither was a brown-eyed girl, or could imagine what Woodstock was like. But they were girls that he did not birth, that he did not father, and that intrigued him. Neither their father, nor their teacher, he liked his status before them. And they liked their status before him.

Lily said, "Hey, Stan, just call me Lady Lily." Her thighs tense and long, as they crossed in Stan's imagination. "What's my life?" a boy with tight jeans beamed in. It was a sensual symphony of sorts. A community was born that included Stan.

A service to the universal holy communion of school and song, he did not say "Welcome kids in the name of Jesus, the Savior of your world." Instead, he sang Van Morrison, then, suddenly, the cords of community were felt in the smell of that song. The Van Morrison comforted the kids, in their sorrows, and it served as a consolation of sorts to them as kids often ignored by adults. Some, knowing Van's work, bridged even better memories of their actual fathers, and some sidled up next to Stan, seeking an adult surrogate.

Sacred and Profane

He had heard as he was starting this dream a chant he had heard thousands of Sundays, the Apostle's Creed. "I believe in the Holy Spirit, the communion of saints, the forgiveness of sins." His dream was being selective, skipping some beats in the creed, like Van Morrison does in his songs that he hums.

During this dream, his son, the music man, played the central role.

Stan's son, six foot two, explained the dream within the dream. His son was recalling a lecture he had from a literature professor during his first and only semester at Suffolk Community College. The lecture broke down the segments of Ralph Waldo Emerson's "Freedom and Fate" essay.

The father, the dreamer, says only a few words during the entire dream: "Stop, why does this matter?" He says it two times, but never gets an answer from his son. Instead of an answer, the son says to the father: "Hey, dad, listen to Van the Man, he has all your answers."

But the music man goes on, lifting themselves up in the clouds with his father.

He says, "Emerson suggests we are all overboard at sea, in a turbulent sea, and while we are aware, all we can really do is look at the eyeballs of the others in the waves."

With that, the music stops, but the dream goes on becoming milky and wet, and perhaps full of a sea that involved both whisky and other women.

Suddenly, they both are in an operating room watching spinal surgery.

The place is immaculate, like an ultra-altar. Small marble steps, plenty of mirrors and gold. Here Stan is feeling the church's Polish prayers of intercession. Someone, the priest perhaps, but it is too dark to tell, says: "You cannot earn a living without realizing that the internet gives writers and music men new ways to earn new revenue streams."

How strange, how basic. It causes Stan to wonder: Here in America what is more important: money or the magic of music?

Stan wanted to say. "The Lord be with you. And also with you. Lift up your hearts." But he could not. He was frozen in this dream with his son, a son who seldom really spoke with Stan from ages 15 to 17. Then it got milky again.

Somehow, when he awakens from this dream, Stan concludes that his only son will never earn a real living. Stan feels low, like a pirate without any booty, like a commuter by train to Manhattan each morning. He feels tired when he wakes up from this family dream. He puts on his working pants, a starched blue jean, declaring to only himself: "I'm looking forward to catching the girls swing at the wiffle ball."

This is the only night dream Stan has for about a month where he is not flying, except at first, slowly ascending up to the cloud with his son. It was more like an elevator than Stan's usual horizontal, remarkably fast night-flying.

This is the only dream where he is not in the deep past, but with current family members. It is a very confusing dream about family, and about music. Confused, he wants to get to work doing the things he knows have meaning.

Eating Lunch at Home

Stan always makes it home for lunch. He is full of life when he gets there.

The school is a mere eight minutes from home. This was like in Europa, and Poland, and he felt it essential. Eat lunch at home. Be near home. His wife has Polish music on when he arrives, and lunch always ready. He is a modern man, a lucky man. Even the coffee is hot, waiting for him in his favorite mug.

Stan's wife always started the lunch with this, as if every lunch was at a beach in a soft wind and spring: "May the grace of Christ our Savior and the Father's boundless love, with the Holy Spirit near, rest upon us and our family." He did not need to say Amen. It was implied. Stan and his wife were lovers since teen years. They kept the faith.

Today, lunch is not unlike a typical lunch. There is the mustard on the sandwich, and the cheese, and there is the meat. Only the mix varied. And there is the warm beer, as well. Warm beer does not hurt his teeth.

The lunch never went over thirty-five minutes, and then straight back to work.

Eating lunch, over time, offered Stan a new theory of being human. Something to look through that was basic about the nature of love, about tears and laughter, and about our procession toward death.

Stan stumbled onto this new theory by digging near the secrets of Joseph's weekend heart, while cleaning his second home. Every month, usually within the first five days, Stan cleans on the Long Island weekend home of a New York University Professor Joseph. (Joseph does not use his last name in front of Stan.) They talked constantly, as Joseph was at home with Stan, and Stan was intrigued by the professor's voice.

From chats with Professor Joseph, Stan knew that biology made his life possible, and that food maintained his strength and drive. Nothing more, Joseph claimed, there is nothing more than this biology. Stan knew better.

Stan remained, nonetheless, quiet and respectful to the world-travelling professor of neuroscience. Stan knew, from changing the diapers of his kids, that something bigger than himself enabled his procession towards death while enabling a lovely inner life, of thoughts and dreams, of longing and desire. That was the key to faith, not the nervous system, Stan felt.

He felt this something eternal in his kids, and in their play, that he could experience himself this way, and in dreams. It was how Stan and his family saw the world. He really wanted to ask the professor more about his faith in flatworms and spinal cords. But he did not dwell on this impossibility. The professor was busy even during his weekend at home, and that required Stan to take his thoughts private and internal. This was more wondrous than confrontation about faith.

Stan, instead, thought about the days he had to miss lunch with his wife. How he wolfed down peanut-butter-and-jelly sandwiches those days in ten minutes. No Polish music, no conversation. He felt half-human during those wifeless lunches. Stan wondered why Joseph never went shopping, and never mentioned a wife or family. This got Stan thinking again about Joseph's claim that it all boils down to biology.

Stan remembered his grandfather warned him about eating too much. The man said in broken English: "Stan, do not overeat! You do not want to make your belly bigger than your view of your own pecker." That was something Stan kept in mind as he feasted. It was necessary to have enough excess but not too much. That was the question over lunch, nothing more.

Stan felt he knew so much more than biology. He felt it when his wife wore a new floral blouse, and deliberately forget to button a few of them during his lunch visits. Wisdom like that for Stan felt spiritual, not nervous.

Stan summed up his gentle disagreement with Joseph one weekend by pointing out the recyclable bag from Hannaford supermarket. Stan pointed out the motto on the side of the reuseable bag, with a smile: "More waves fish trees birds; less plastic. Be bold. Bring a bag."

Stan said to Joseph, "That's wisdom."

Joseph said, "That's garbage."

Rethinking youth. Feeling again the steep musicality in good memories.

Be not afraid of joy.

THIRD SEQUENCE: STEPPING BACK INTO FAMILY AND FRIENDS

His dream is about the loss of his lifelong friend Walter Freeman. Walter, another scientist turned world traveler, proved so much more than Professor Joseph. Like all great dreams, this Freeman dream assembled feelings about the death of Walter, the new kids Stan was finding wonderful at school, and a bunch of other fragments from his recent days.

These other fragments included magical feelings in flight as he flew over in sleep what he witnessed at the Wild Center during the open big White Tent celebration of Walter's life in Tupper Lake. As he flew, one of the things he noticed in the dream was the recurrent message on the Hannaford supermarket bags the attendants used during the ceremony to bring in the feast for all. "More waves fish trees birds; less plastic. Be bold. Bring a bag."

All great Stan dreams have three or four lived fragments of a day, or a few days, compiled into one dream narrative. Maybe it was better to note that the dark compliments or compilations were more like compressions of fragments. The tension was felt in the compression of the dream, its speed, not just its surrounding darkness. This dream was clearly working out his feelings about Walter's death.

But this time the dream was not in the deep past.

Instead, the dream became about a ceremony Stan and his wife had witnessed at the Wild Center in Tupper Lake, New York. Its first message was: "Let us go forth in peace, in the name of Christ. Amen." There were a series of other compressed messages, such as right up front in the dream.

The dream poem boldly stated:

"The Doctors are Right,

> "At seventy and a quarter-years old, we will rent a big tent for a celebration at Lake Tupper's Wild Center, with friends and colleagues from afar, for their joy in seeing the otters and the big Adirondack trees.
>
> "They will come in shorts, sport shirts, and the women in grey.
>
> "They, the women in grey, will be more beautiful, and smart and social than during work. For at seventy, only the imagination is real.

As if all aligned, they all dream in union during the ceremony, claiming: Walter Freeman was a force in nature. Even after his brain hemorrhage—Walter was a person of solid faith; returning to his strong beliefs even after watching a fellow hiker fall to his death.

Then the dream moves into a slower motion, like a fine lyric made of silk fabric:

"Walter would announce
German numbers as he ascended
Steps; and in his youth, he
Reached exceptional pinnacles
As rock climber and hiker.
We watched his still-old worn hiking boots
at the Wild Center Ceremony,
Under the big White Tent,
With his minister neighbors
And a vast array of loved ones.
They did not move—those worn boots—as we imagined
His ascents in recall and picture."

Suddenly he felt meaning and belief in the dream poem:

"Walter rose from a replacement
Of the retaining piece of metal
In his skull, when the Minister
Asked: 'Arise, Mr. Walter.' And he did."
I sat with his minister at the lunch,
Spellbound by further tales of Walter Freeman,
His lurid vivid dreams, his engine of faith."

Stan awoke, telling his wife: "Come one, come all off from the long string of winds and turns that shape this magnificent Lake

Tupper, New York, even if you chose to miss the ceremony for the otters and trees."

Stan's wife had no clear clue what he was talking about. She gave Stan a big hug. She got their breakfast ready.

Upon focusing on his breakfast, the words of the funeral march in streaming stopped, like the abrupt end of a poem.

Stan's dreams often gave him a better job as they ended. Yet what is strangest, he loved his actual job upon awakening. Eating lunch was his forte. At mid-day he was at his prime. Thinking about what he learned from his dreams was his self-appointed daily ritual. After dreaming about the poem dreamt about Walter's death, he started thinking about how he would spend his remaining days.

Stan's mind was perhaps a bit uneducated, yet it was fast and furious. From friend to work and back, he thought. From life to death, and death to life.

He was no longer a teenager, no longer middle-aged. The long sensual middle had brought him a puzzle in his head to ponder after Joseph and Walter. It said: "Stan, most of the time I want you to be a happy child in this new world of America with a large family, and once a week with an adequate cash flow." He felt this puzzle gave him a license to grow, like a successful re-entry from space. There was no specific end in sight, but he felt the end nearing.

The Next Days and Nights

The events of the recent past made Stan seek more. In the past, it was enough to see the black-footed ferret, and smile. Or to notice on PBS TV the strange grey eyes of the Florida panther—and smile again. In the past, he was sufficient watching the beach's piping plover, grayfish, and small-masked birds. But after the service in honor of the death of his friend Walter Freeman, he sought more from his life.

While he had trained his first decades upon leaving Poland to do more with less, now he wanted more range, more reach, more longing. This new drive was not quite like the many cowboys he admired, and sometimes mock-mimicked in the films, always going westward. Instead, he had become more like his faithful turtle at night, Stan's nose pointed upward in a joyful pursuit of where the bubbles led.

This scared and prompted. This alerted and egged onwards.

He slapped himself several times, to kick-start his morning coffee. Was he more now like a wolf or a panther during his day, angered by the death of his friend? If so, no one noticed. He wanted things to level off some, to stabilize. But they did not. He was still Stan the man but entering higher orbits.

His mind now exceeded the speed of Van Morrison, his wife, and the death of his friend combined. He could jump around in analogue like a man floating, like a turtle swimming as if he owned the currents, free to roam.

His next set of work days led to robust nights, and all dream nights to a more and more robust work day.

He had, despite his standing, become a Möbius strip, the endless number eight.

He asked himself:

> What is joy? A set of bubbles or a jet in flight?
> What is enough in our world of turbulent seas, waves on waves, that hit Robert Moses Beach with force in storm and in calm?
> What can the little boy in the janitor become with additional decades in his life?

Stan had asked these questions before, alone, with his rational self. But after the recent events he found better answers in his dreams. As a turtle hobbles forward on land, he was paid for his chores. Yet in his dreams the chores become lessons and cheers, and his isolation becomes a floating journey shared with greater portions of humanity. This was the big reveal. A choice made across a thousand nights.

There was so much now to reflect on: from the birth of his daughter, the growth of his elder son, to the emergence of his new second son as a musician.

A Dream of Milk, Whisky, and Women

The spout of the dream said "Pour!"

Pour milk. Pour reduced fat in women. Pour the awakening of the first tastes of the sharp whiskies of his youth, those lean women leaning against him on the Long Island railroad in his early years, and his wife's vitamin-enriched milks. "Thanks for choosing them" each gulp, he said in this dream.

By pouring it all, Stan the man is no longer poor, but enriched, like a Duke basketballer drunk at the free throw line. Swoosh. Swoosh. Gulp into greatness, the dream said.

Before the grasping crowd, tugging at his gym shorts, now he could taste in the dream the milk of his own mother in Poland. He grew in size in the dream, back in Poland but beyond it, with the farm cows of youth but also the long sensual middle years growing up, plus the manure and the stink in his trousers. "How did those years of youth to middle age jive by so fast?" he asked in this dream.

His dream now turned to being ten years old. It did not matter that he already felt like an adult at ten, hands on his hips before the girls. He had already convinced all American girls within his reach of his bike that being 8 years old was magical, like the infinite number 8 itself.

Yet now at ten, his taste was for those becoming shapely, and his dream ended in this endless succession of ejaculations. Most of his dreams started with something building, like an erection, but this one ended in a set of ejaculations that proved clean, and acceptable, to both his mother and the girls, quite remarkable really. He was seeing double that morning, but he still smiled at the thought of the dream about whisky, women, and milk mixed into one, as images of a Pope were pushed way back in his dream, back as far as a Polish dungeon.

Travelling Insurance

Stan cleaned the offices, each weekend, of one of Long Island's prominent companies that offered global travel insurance. This earned him the extra cash they all longed for in America.

For more than two decades, this set of travel insurance agents offered coverage in the event of harm, both in flight and far-away places like Rio and Morocco, places of fancy to Stan.

While he cleaned an empty office on Saturday near noon, he looked around at the papers and the payment records left out and saw in them the immense amount of travel these Long Island and Manhattan folks did.

This firm excelled at meeting these endowed people—folks like Joseph and Walter—and then charged them for some assurances.

Some even had annual "blanket assurances." He wished he had thought of that payment concept, and made blanket-cleaning deals.

It made Stan smile to think about travel insurance. He did not understand the complex calculations of national risk, travel risk, and payment. But he saw in the documents a phrase "family wealth target." This got him dreaming at work.

Stan imagined he was invited to become a family wealth target, probably because of the mint his older son paid for his saxophone. In fantasy, they were enjoying themselves on the side roads of South Africa, playing music, when they were targeted.

Once, when picking up his cash live (they always wanted not to mail the checks, they did not want to know his home address for some reason), Stan asked: "Once at the firm, do your best people stay, or do they themselves travel or move to your Manhattan headquarters....?"

The payment clerk looked at Stan for a long time, and answered: "Sir, I am afraid that is above my head and pay grade."

What a strange, strange answer. Stan walked away wondering if he left piss or poop on his shoe or something like that.

It never cross Stand's faithful mind that soon this travel insurance company would be slammed shut by a fraudulent claims department. Zoom. Boom. Closed. He wasn't fired as much as they expired.

Stan had to act fast, and through a dance company, he found a replacement set of bills for the travel insurance client.

Travel insurance and the dance of discovery were related in Stan's mind from then on. This replacement job made Stan underline his reliance on faith. He was never really deprived of cash on Long Island.

Family and faith.

Old world and new.

Old Testament and New.

He had grown before himself. Stan no longer had any trouble with these dual things. Travel and discovery in his life was easy, not troubled.

The travel insurance scam unsettled him. The Walter Freeman ceremony reassured him, and his new forms of longing brought delight and an answer in joys. One after the other.

His family was happy with where he was. He was happy with simple back-to-basic things. He was now happy to find a substitute in the dance studio near Montauk Highway, mature intelligent women in tights, swinging into dance for longevity.

He felt sane, lucky, and rich when this fell onto his lap. What a lucky fool he remained. A sense of something much bigger than remorse and regret and loss now surrounded him.

Be not afraid of loss.

FOURTH SEQUENCE: NEAR THE THRESHOLD OF JOY

There had always been a sensual side to being a janitor. Some days and weeks offered complexities, and too many things crashed into his head as they neared the end of the school year.

Out in the schoolyard this day, Stan finds a two-page eulogy about Walter Freeman on the schoolyard driveway, where the yellow buses wait in idle. It is, in a strange way, a map to his own heart. The sheet takes him places, where he thinks about his own death with a clear mind.

He has no clue how this eulogy got here. Perhaps his kids stuffed it in his car from Tupper Lake, and when he opened his trunk to get the vacuum supplementary cleaner he preferred, the sheet flew out into the schoolyard.

The short sheet was written by a close friend of the deceased. The writer was direct and honest, stronger than most. Out in this schoolyard Stan reads the sheet slowly, several times rereading it, despite being distracted by some disobedient students he chose to keep an eye on.

Stan brought it home to read to his wife. His wife said, "Honey this Walter Freeman has always reminded me of you, but at least you are still alive!" This is some of what Stan found in the eulogy said in a heartfelt and exacting fashion. It is hard to write about death, but even harder, Stan thought, to write about the death of a dear friend.

The sheet of Walter's lifelong friend said:

> "Walter's earthly life is complete; a short reflection on it must be incomplete. Chemist, mountaineer, author, singer. Those four words get parts of Walter Freeman, but not all.
>
> "Like the driving force behind early Renaissance exploration of the world, Walter led many an adventurous trip like Henry the Navigator.
>
> "Henry was like Walter, and Walter like Henry. Both had that vision and determination of an avid unremitting explorer. Henry launched Portugal on its unprecedented century of discovery. Walter did not find the Cape. Walter found his resolve in the Adirondack Mountains. Walter lived hope, and hope found in family and friends and adventure."

Stan pauses in his reading of that stray sheet. Stan looked again at his wife's warm face. The sheet was more music than eulogy. There was poetry in this everyday celebration of his friend Walter.

There was an urge to urinate, so Stan got up, and he resisted some, wanting to know the end of the thought path in his reading.

He got up reluctantly, not to interrupt the magic before his wife. Stan made his way to the bathroom in the dark. Rather rapidly, Stan disciplined himself to return to read the sheet from Walter's friend:

In the sheet, the friend continued....

> "Walter could be unfiltered. Forty-five years ago when I told Walter of my planned marriage to Maureen, he lamented the prospect, noting that many of his friends, upon entering married life, 'deteriorated.'
>
> "But by 2008, when he married for the first time at age 70, his attitude had changed. Walter had the grace to rise above his minor foibles and major challenges. He was resilient, largely because he was a man of faith. I'll tell a concluding story.
>
> "Six of us set out to climb a 600-foot Adirondack cliff. Walter and I roped together. We and another pair had reached the top and watched the third pair coming up the last few feet. A hand-hold came loose, Bill fell sixty feet, broke his neck, and soon died. In the following hours and days, we survivors had different reactions. Some were in denial; some swore off technical climbing from that moment.
>
> "Walter, of course, mourned our loss, but he was otherwise at peace, and soon returned to climbing. He trusted that Bill was now in a better place, and that the rest of us

had been spared for some reason. These beliefs came from his faith in God."

Stan's wife embraced Stan. They understood each other, and they understood the sheet word by word.

These comments by Don, friend of Walter Freeman, seared into Stan's mind like the time when, on rare occasion, he saw a masterpiece painting in a museum.

During the prior part of his workday, when he was first reading the fine eulogy, he saw in the corner of his eye, between the yellow buses, a girl—was it Grace or Lily?—giving a schoolboy a blow job.

Out in the Schoolyard

He saw her held head bobbing up and down, and the sweetened face of the boy.

Stan did not know what to do then. And he did not tell his wife this event either, while reading to her about Don and Walter. Was this a failure?

He knew the school buses would leave in a matter of minutes. He waited. They finished, and the buses in a military regiment moved on.

Life itself was a joke, Stan thought, smiling in thinking about the pleasure of his youth.

He would be home again that night, with his wife, and that would be everything.

As he waited for the last bus to leave, Stan saw again with his vivid memory Bosch's "Ship of Fools" painting, something he had not seen for years. When he first saw the painting it disturbed him, a backyard table being perverted by misuse.

But Stan now saw the picture as a miniature summary of his recent travels in his mind. Although he did not know what inspired such a painting, Stan felt life a grand joke, watching the girl and watching the boy.

Stan felt the human soul loving and good. This was life. And the ceremony of the wonderful commemoration of Walter Freeman was another kind of life.

He chose not to report the girl or the boy.

Commuting Home

While commuting home that day, he drove slower than usual. Some of the yellow school buses beat him down Higbie Lane, which was rare. While most of his life had been fast-forward, he was learning to pause, and to enjoy even more.

Yet despite his cautious slowness, he was disturbed in his routine.

He avoided two accidents by chance, one with a motorbike jumping a light, and another from a big Red RAM truck. "Who needs a RAM truck?" he asked himself. Stan missed that truck by inches, by seconds. It would have made him a Walter Freeman.

Was God telling him something he did not yet understand? He understood family, walking to work, enjoying work, being with the kids at the high school

Later that evening, he saw on the evening news a few additional Long Island commuter accidents.

He, by chance, remained one of the lucky ones.

But he could not erase the image of the girl, the image of his poem dream, Walter Freeman's boot watching the friend die, the deep honesty of Walter's friend and his careful commentary on what was done and what remained. These events constituted a different feeling than he was used to.

Stan felt glad most days were not as complicated.

Back at Home

Stan was a simple man, a modern man, in full.

He did not need to take big risks to be happy.

While enjoying the great wealth evident in the homes of some of his weekend clients, he felt he had made it the right way, without feeling the weight of too many obligations.

Returning home to his accordion, he contemplated, in the spirit of Joseph, his instrument. Neither its cost, nor its label from Poland, seemed to matter now. For after watching the events of the prior days, the instrument itself mattered. How did it work? Why did it feel so alive, without a nervous system?

Stan was not going to take apart his instrument, but he wondered about this bellow-driven box. There must be some set of reeds inside the frame, where he can be a band at once without needing others? He decided he really did not need to know why it works, as his fingers went up and down on both keyboards.

On the right-side keyboard, he plays a melody from his memory, as Stan does not know how to read music. And on his left keyboard he is another man, making entirely different sounds and chords.

It was simply magic, this box.

There was joy in lifting that box, that instrument, and he kept the keys of the instrument clean and lasting.

When Stan played the accordion in his backyard, the parrot in his kitchen started to sing, and his German Shepherd dog paid attention. What more would one man want?

Despite all the troubling events of recent days, back at home, with his magical accordion, and his family, Stan felt grand again.

Eating Dinner with Wife and Kids

Like everyman, he wanted to defy the coming of death just a little longer, like an old dog in heat. Death, wearing expensive pantaloons, was in his dreams again. She was coming near, breathing on his face as he tried to sleep. He was a soldier boy in his deepest dreams, wearing Polish peasant warrior clothes and buckles.

Down in the basement of his dreams was a picture of what the Reds did to a Polish officer during the wars in 1920, more than a hundred years before. The naked man was hanged upside down, beaten, cut, and tortured with a sharp stick until he died before an audience of neighbors.

Stan only wanted a family audience when he died. The words that mistakenly swirled in his head, whenever he thought through his own death, were, "I'd rather be vanquished by family than famished by fame." It did not quite add up to common sense, but it was how he felt.

English would always be his second language, and words like "vanquished" and "famished" and "fame" joined in his imagination like books stacked near him in the school library shelves. There was a persistence to his memory of his past nation, Poland; and that is why he often mispronounced or misused certain words in English.

Alice was the girl who came to like that about Stan.

There were several reasons why his immediate ancestors in Poland, being peasants, resisted the Red Army. His uncles spoke of it in terms of remembered cities: Tambov, Riazan, Tula, Kaluga, Smolensk, Vitebsk, Pskov, Novgorod, Mogileve—even parts of Moscow itself saw Polish rebels, and bands of peasants with harrows, spades, and axes.

Death was more remote in America. Death had been sanitized in a sense, in clean hospitals not visible before families and in farms.

Stan's family had a small stone house on its farm for several hundred years. Alice, again, liked that tale from Stan. She was a remarkable young woman.

When he heard about the tales of Kaluga, he confused it with Alice's aspirations to wind up at Cornell high above the Lake of Cayuga. In the box of his Uncle Steve, Stan remembered actual pictures of the torture of the Poles. It was his people's tragedy. There was no need for further reading on that subject.

The way he fixed his need to defy death was to eat dinner with his wife and kids. The great wars in his family memory could be suspended that way, with strawberries fresh from his favorite farms on Long Island, and with music.

Just like igneous rock forms inside the earth's surface, the crystals of Stan's memories of Poland and war formed inside his heart, its beats at work, and inside his dreams. You could not separate one from the other, rock and heart, crystal and memory. Yet by eating dinner with wife and kids, he would somehow forget and forgive. He could think again about the moments before him.

Taking a Nap before the Game

For Stan, there was a deliberate ambiguity he felt after any fine meal.

He was happy, but it made him want to nap. The feeling encompassed both the divine in digestion and the erotic. He wondered if others had this feeling after any large meal. He wondered if this pleasant fog was like God's prelude to feeling ready for death.

Falling again into an afternoon dream journey, he became Sir Richard Burton, the British intelligence gatherer. His son had told Stan about Sir Richard Burton, after taking intelligence training at community school for a Defense Department job in New Mexico. Stan sent himself in this dream to the wild tribes and plains to collect information for his next meal. He did not go as a British officer, nor as a commissioner, but as a native, a tattered dirty-looking dervish who could avoid the wars of certainty to become venerated for his simplicity. Jates and Jews, Polish Gypsies, and Camel men and women understood him in this dream.

Mixing his anxiety about Polish prosecution with the immediate Muslim dream rites on the way to Mecca before him, he realized one thing: When one realizes that each man or woman before you is a person, and that we all must make our calculations about the risk of immediate violent death at the hands of angry mobs and guards of insanity in politics or markets, you must wonder if the difference between survival and death boils down to a matter of a few feet and a few seconds.

Fate and freedom were, after all, sisters in the common crimes of a day and night.

He remembered in the dream the close calls he had while driving. What made that second of delay that avoided the oncoming truck?

He now saw no fewer than five men had fallen down and died upon the highway; exhausted and famished, they dragged themselves out to let others pass. There was a dignity and beauty in how, like a deer hit in the road, they dragged themselves away from the marching crowds in pilgrimage. The spectacle showed Stan how easy it is to die in these places. Each man simply suddenly staggered, fell as if shot; and after a brief convulsion and conversion, lay as still as marble on the roadside.

All was confusion again when Alice appeared as a Persian girl.

When he awoke, Stan told his son he was ready to watch the basketball game, with potato chips and a British gin.

After such an affable afternoon nap, British gin was far better than his usual beer.

Be not afraid of family, good fortune, and friends.

LAST SEQUENCE: STEPPING INTO THE LIBRARY THAT LASTS

Stan lamented his children's addictions to technology.

They could not sit still long enough to watch a 48-minute basketball game with him. He felt in his soul that this was the real whole loss of contemporary life—inattention. You cannot experience the devil or true bliss if you are distracted.

Stan felt their reliance on playing on their handhelds during the game, and this devotion to several kinds of technology at once, did not serve a fulfilling substitute for what he used to enjoy as "game time." He did not make a message out of this, instead a point of discovery. All this angered him a bit, especially when his basketball team was losing, horribly.

Yet all he had to do was switch the channel of his memory to that of Alice and Lily, and he'd forget his small irritations at his kids and their handhelds. He loved deeply his wife, yet he found he would also love his dreams and memories.

Stan had a rage regarding technology. He believed in the human soul. He had faith it would all work out. His team still lost that night. He went immediately after the game to sleep, seeking a dream path to resolutions, choosing not to open the book he had received for Christmas called *The Arabian Nights*.

He never had the patience to open Sir Richard Burton's heavy illustrated English translation of *The Arabian Nights*. This was one of the hundreds of books whose binders he touched in the high school library. Stan felt he knew these books in touching their binders and reading their first three pages. He did not need to lift that heavy one at night after all. For him, moving back to basics was being aware they were there, and that was enough.

This morning, after the lost game, he felt earnest. He felt hemmed in, for some reason, feeling like an older man at sea. Alone in a boat at sea. In a fashion showing his mounting age, he chose to read before work a second gift book, this one recently given by his daughter.

His daughter had bought him Hemingway's memoir, and he liked the idea of "*A Moveable Feast*." He read: "A girl came in the café and sat by herself at a table near the window. She was very pretty with a face fresh as a newly minted coin if they minted coins in smooth flesh with rain-freshened skin, and her hair black as a crow's wing and cut sharply and diagonally across her cheek."

This Hemingway must have known his own Alice, he thought, and then Stan got straight back to work. Her hair was as black as a crow's wing, and her flighty ways embodied her pretty face. But even Hemingway never got a chance to watch her round the bases in those wiffle ball games. Stan was again content, he did not need to order rum, only memories.

Sleeping with Tom Wolfe Senior

The student who hung with Obama's daughter also knew Tom Wolfe, the literary giant from Manhattan. Stan did not know her name, he thought of her as "the one who knew the famous." She seemed to like talking to Stan about these celebrities brought into her parents' realm so early in her life on Long Island.

Alice said she hoped some day she could sleep with Tom Wolfe, while he was wearing his white jacket. Alice told this to the student who hung with Obama's daughter. They felt it reminded them of a Van Morrison jingle. They laughed with that youthful abandon Stan had trouble understanding.

He concluded it was more about longing than anything. They both knew Tom Wolfe Senior was much older than they were, and they knew him to be near death. Yet they still longed for his imagined attention, as if a great man's books could awaken new life in them.

As Stan aged, his vivid dreams became less about drives and shades and dark areas and more about actual words in his head. He remembered Ben Franklin saying as Poor Richard: "Old boys have their playthings as well as young ones; the only difference is the price." That was 1733, and now is now, still true as we age.

Stan was now ready to stand tall in his dreams about writing, and books. Bold writers in white jackets and leather shoes with their grand style attracted him. Why shouldn't they? He was entitled. He did not need to imagine sleeping with these authors, just being near their books in the high school library proved enough. He often went back to those books to calm himself, after a schoolteacher had looked past him.

Stan was not a writer. But he had become a reader, mostly self-taught after Poland.

He had read Freud and Proust, James and Joyce, at least their book jackets in the school library when no one was bothering to pace his work. No one stopped him in America. In most of the books he found attractive, he read the first three pages.

There were many great books to touch and—as he flipped through them in this little West Islip high school library—he felt part of the much larger world.

There were the cluster of adventure books: George Vancouver on the Pacific, James Jenkins on British naval adventures, David Roberts on Egypt and the Holy Lands. These books were available to Stan in a quick flip of the illustrations.

Next he found the cluster of famous-people books: Winston Churchill on his war, Charles Darwin explaining how simple beginnings became the most beautiful forms evolved, Francisco Goya on his great antiwar manifesto in both artful drawings and forceful prose. Stan felt these great books also within his grasp.

But he had serious trouble grasping the vast array of novels the West Islip librarians had collected for the kids. Upon thumbing their spines, these narratives seemed to have too much in them for him to categorize about loss, adventure, or history. Thereby, he felt them more vast, more difficult to subsume in a quick pass. *Dune* was much more than about sand dunes, and *The Catcher in the Rye* more than about rye bread.

Now he was dreaming about Moby Dick, Ahab in turbulence, even about Tom Wolfe's *The Bonfire of the Vanities* as a father figure in a white jacket. All the greats were jumbled together as a person who took a Great Books' year-long seminar in one week, one dream.

Books in his school's small library were all he needed, as he aged at what seemed like a quicker pace than in his 50s. His wrists were getting arthritic.

These books in the small lovely and clean library bridged his sense of the deep past. He was content to know where they stood in this school's library. Blurring the lines between reality, memory, and imagination, many library books had become to him like his most favored dreams. Yet they stayed in place for him, and the shelves, and he liked that he could go back to them again and again. Blurring the lines between reality, memory, and imagination, his time dusting in the library became a layered, contemplative supreme time in his days.

This reading of the first three pages of great books causes Stan to regurgitate in his dreams what he read, often in a jumbled way that would make critics cringe. As things fall apart in the real world, he has a rebirth, a renaissance, in his dream life where fragments fall together.

Books bridge Stan to a deeper past, far away in different ages; yet books also strike him like sharks in the shallows of today.

That is why he chose not to report the girl or the boy. He did not want to confront pretentious idiots. Why he became reborn.

He thinks this time about Alice again, but from a lyric by Van Morrison his daughter often sang:

> "Hey, where did we go, days when the rains came
> Down in the hollow, playing a new game
> Laughing and a-running, hey, hey
> Skipping and a-jumping
> In the misty morning fog with our, our hearts a-thumping
> And you, my brown eyed girl
> You, my brown eyed girl."

Without knowing much about this girl's actual life, he travelled many places with Alice while sleeping. Alice was more than his wonderland in his dreams. She was active, popping, and happy at it. With no guilt, nor deceit, nor hope of actuality, Stan often dreamt of Alice, or was it sometimes also Lily, Lady Lily?

When he dreamt about Tom Wolfe he felt near an actual American father, not his father from Poland. Tom, the legend, was flamboyant, funny, and fair.

It was Alice who had the brown eyes. Echt American. Alice was the one, his priest once told him, and did not know why, that the Yiddish word "echt" meant "true to form", and that ironically, the Germans borrowed "echt" from the Jews. Alice was the real McCoy, although neither German, Jewish, nor Irish. Alice was Alice, and frankly that is what he loved about her in his dream and sleeping life.

He felt justified in his sleeping life by being near Alice.

She was the future. He was the past.

She was radiant. He was dusty.

She had perhaps most of a century before her. He was built on the ruins of old cultures in conflict.

Dreaming Again

The choice is ours. Either things fall apart, or we sum up all the dreams and coin it grand. The choice is ours.

To the success of our hopeless causes, pray—which is the other way to phrase it. Yes, the choice is ours. Stan always knew that because his mother taught him so.

These perfectly harmonized twin dramas—the trial hatreds, and the summary halo—are informed by an awareness capable of encompassing at once both the destruction of human history to sin, and the transcendence of individual will in nature, among all the competition, grief, and compulsions of the soul.

The strong men in literature, from Africa to Asia, Stan's dream travels suggest: They all know this. Even the people and fine women of his old world, and the new world—the bitter frontier of Long Island, the people of Long Island, can know this. While a vivid imagination greets his every day and every dream, he is the same as every man, and likes it. Gloriously gifted by the obvious, and the profane, his janitor's sweep is all. He will clean both piety and sin, the complex and the needy.

Stan still feels something vitally wrong in Oz. The temples and temptations of his past are too compelling to completely ignore individual and family bliss. And the rest is family, the meals and deals of the immediate family, and the family of men and women.

"Let me write now on the walls of death," he said at the beginning of what felt like a summary dream. He was beginning again to think and feel not of the genesis of things but the ending of things.

Murder, rape, fathomless guilt, moral decline—refractions of genetic ailments, all these were scanned by the feelings at the beginning of this new dream. But it was the middle that was most dramatic, like in a fabulous poem. Commentators look for ambiguity in the middle of our dream life, but in this case, the sheer intensity of the middle of the dream was beyond commentary. It felt like hell.

He built a fire in the backyard stone fire pit his daughter had built for him, knowing he liked losing himself to the stare of a good fire. But in this dream, he had to sacrifice his only daughter.

Careful dreamers know how close they come to murder in their dreams, knife raised, with the daughter's athletic limbs biblical in their submission. His dream response was not reassuring.

Instead of killing his daughter on command, he chose to talk with her, about the near misses in his life, how his death wore pantaloons. She smiled in the dream, like she did in real life, knowing her dad limited. The dream ended again abruptly.

He was a little civilization built within a set of larger ones. As his dream pursued the laws of completion, he realized that his God demanded justice rather than sacrifice. Trivialized by the near murder, he awoke.

Walking to Work

Simple truths and vital lies. Kites and hot-air balloons. Stan thought, and explored, what he called simple parallels, analogues by another name. For the fun of it, he was going to float free of concern as he walked. Today he was going to take the long way to walk to work.

He never saw things without this binocular view, having bad eyes to begin with.

Overall he liked most of the people he had met in life, and felt them neither a full liar nor a full truth-teller. Stan went back to basics with each human, knowing before he asked them that their minds could protect themselves against anxiety by dimming awareness. When Stan met them in the post office or the supermarket he gave them the benefit of the doubt. Instead of liars or truth-tellers, he thought of them as either kites or hot-air balloons.

The kites were more at the mercy of the world of events, blowing in the wind. The hot-air balloons, often engineers or technicians, felt more certain, but often for the wrong reasons. The hot-air people forced nuance onto their audiences like a novelist might think they are offering jam, but are offering linoleum toast instead.

To him, humans were both liars and truth-tellers at once. That is what made his life as an observer fun. This helped him avoid some of the professional bad habits of self-importance and self-deception, Alice once told him.

Today he was taking long agitated strides to work. He did not have the time, today, to allow blind spots, zones of blocked attention, or self-deception. He was done with depression.

He was nearing the end of something.

Over the last few weeks, the top Lit teacher in the high school, a teacher who kept all the girls alert and all the boys challenged, had talked too much about the heavy downpour of prose written by Henry James. Yet in Stan's walking mind, he learned a good deal sweeping outside of this Lit teacher's room, that he wanted to digest during this walk to work. In this way, Stan was an excellent student, simple but covering the whole map. The Lit teacher helped him conclude something about writing and janitorial work.

Henry James, like the Portuguese adventurer Henry the Navigator, embellished much in his travels. That much Stan knew from the lectures. James's prose was not so much dusty as heavy, laden like a wet cloth that Stan drops on some floors to get them ready before cleaning. His books were swollen, like a horse penis in heat.

Henry the Navigator is rumored to have had many a prince in his pocket because of his abilities to embellish lands not yet discovered, like James had novel after novel. If the late James lacked reality in his swollen affairs, Henry the Navigator lacked evidence. Yet they both prospered between truth and lies.

Stan did not want to be tethered to the ground. His dream-work was his real work, after all, and his fascination in people as people was the dirty truth. He would study them all day, as they thought him simple and even rude in his directness.

"Vital lies versus simple truths," Stan thought, as he turned by his sister's favorite church, The Lady of Lourdes, off a small mall and past his high school.

When we get back to basics, we are no longer tied to the earth, but instead, swing, thanks to the remarkable length of the ropes of the imagination, in an open box, in the open air. We stay in the common and commodious car of the imagination as we dream, and as we walk, if we want to.

Be not afraid.

AFTERWORD

by Bill Novelli, professor emeritus at the McDonough School of Business at Georgetown University; former CEO of AARP and Porter Novelli. His latest book is *Good Business: The Talk, Fight, Win Way to Change the World.*

Did you finish reading Bruce Piasecki's parable wanting more? I did. I really like Stan the man. He's a very engaging guy, maybe the character for a movie someday—a philosopher with a push broom.

Stan the man, the globe-trotting dreamer, is many things. He's a dreamer, yes. He is also a hero in a quiet, everyman sense of heroism.

He's a school janitor and yet a scholar, having absorbed knowledge by touching the jackets of many books in the school library and reading a few pages of some. Stan is largely invisible in his job, but at the same time liked by kids and told by one of them he has emotional intelligence. Who doesn't want that? He takes some of the kids with him in his dreams.

Stan is a family man who loves his wife devotedly (and with a lusty libido). He revels in his children, although he is annoyed at their short attention spans. He wonders if any kid can sit without cell phone action long enough to watch a basketball game. (Note to Stan: there are 310 million smartphones in America, 95 percent of American teens own one, and the average kid spends about eight hours a day looking at a screen.)

Cicero, the Roman scholar and philosopher, said that if you have a garden and a library, you have everything you need. Stan didn't have a garden, and his library was in his head—from touching those school library books. But he was mostly a contented man.

When I taught ethical leadership in the MBA program at Georgetown, my students' favorite reading was by Clayton Christensen, who asked, "How can I be sure I'll be happy in my career? And how can I be sure my relationships with my spouse and family become an enduring source of happiness?" Christensen's advice was to learn, to be responsible, to contribute to others and to apply your knowledge to the purpose of your everyday life. Stan did that. He had it figured out. He knew joy. Even his accordion brought him joy. He didn't need to know how it worked.

Stan is a man of faith, and the key to his faith is his inner life of thoughts and dreams. He believes in being a good citizen who wishes nations could be more at peace.

He's an immigrant, proud to be an American (his land of the free, where you could attain any goal) despite the ethnic prejudices his family has faced. Benjamin Franklin said about immigration that strangers are welcome; there is room for all. But that was back in 1782. Not so true today.

Above all else, Stan is a dreamer. He dreams well back into history, and his vivid dreams carry him incredible distances. Like explorers who got lost (most apparently did), Stan wandered around the globe.

He's not bogged down by physical laws. Who knows—there may be alternative universes out there with entirely different physics. When Michael Jordan was the world's greatest basket-baller, sports writers sometimes said he defied the laws of phys-ics ("he's pissing on gravity"). So does Stan. And he brings some dreams back with him upon reentry to his very ordinary life. He would often tell his kids what he had learned.

Stan was brave; he wasn't afraid of life, but death was some-thing else. Like most of us—no matter who we are or what we have achieved—Stan thinks a great deal about death. He's not in decline; he sees no end in sight, but he feels the end nearing. Maybe we all feel that way. As Bruce tells us, Stan is in a "proces-sion towards death."

After his friend Walter's demise, and after he found and read a eulogy about Walter, Stan thought more and more about what he wanted from life: more range, more reach, to enter higher orbits. He asked, "What is my life?" He wonders, what's next? He's happy in his work, but aspires to something more.

Stan wanted to defy death just a little longer. What could be more human than that? As Mia Funk said in her Introduction,

Bruce has interwoven themes of morality, legacy, and the enduring significance of the human condition.

A parable, like this one about Stan the man, is a story that is told to illustrate moral and spiritual truth. And Bruce delivers. He tells us that it's a free world and the choice is ours: we can let things fall apart or we can bring them together. We have the ability to create our own destiny. In America, you can be a janitor like Stan or a Harvard physician, and both can come from the same family. But justice must be served. Stan is indeed a man of faith, and he believes that "God demands justice."

And finally, like Stan, we can break the bonds that tether us to the earth. So, dare to dream. There's a world, perhaps many worlds out there. Be not afraid.

Bruce is a storyteller, which is among our oldest traditions. It brings us together. A good story often hinges on change, and on both action and reflection. *Stan the Man* is a good story. It makes us really think about who we are, and who we might be. I can't wait for the movie.

EXCERPTS FROM *DOING MORE WITH ONE LIFE*

In 2014, Bruce Piasecki published *Missing Persons,* a memoir which was re-published in 2024 under the title *Doing More with One Life*. This work of creative nonfiction explores the life-shaping moments in his personal history and imagines what is to come next in a series of well-wrought vignettes. The memoir explores the meaning and power of memory, and offers an opportunity for the reader to pause, reflect, and recount the myriad influences in their own lives.

Following are excerpts from the memoir, selected as fitting accompaniments for the reader to the themes and styles of *Stan the Man*. If you enjoy these passages, please seek out and read the full memoir, which can be found on Amazon and other retailers.

—Peter Lynch

From the Foreword by Jay Parini

This memoir is an eye-opener both for its frankness and for how it fits yet distorts literary traditions.

Throughout, Piasecki takes us on an unexpected journey into a new form of autobiography, a life story projected and reflected. For this most dramatic book proves itself to have deep roots in American and in the Latin American traditions of magical realism. Furthermore, the author overall creates an atmosphere of pragmatic self-awareness.

This comes directly from the realms of modern business, but also indirectly from the wit and ambitions of Ben Franklin. It is this eclectic mix that proves electrifying.

Doing More with One Life is a book about the absences that define our lives, the tears in the fabric that we spend a lifetime trying to repair. Piasecki reshapes his life, rediscovers lost family and friends, and connects to literary ancestors—some of whom, like Walt Whitman, lend a layer of texture and allusion to his prose that makes it not only readable but re-readable.

Piasecki's inventive memoir includes over seventy interrelated vignettes—tiny nuggets of narration that nest within the larger narrative arc as the author describes his growing self-awareness, a slowly widening sense of the world. The vignettes move in a roughly chronological fashion, but some of them play back and repeat certain themes and motifs—as with key characterizations of the author's long-dead father, Walter, his generous mother Lillian, his lovely daughter Colette, and his strong wife Varlissima. These characters dance in his head, and their voices underpin his own. They appear and disappear, flash and fade.

This is a fresh and highly readable contribution to the art of autobiography. It has narrative thrills and the frissons of poetic insights. By accretion and artful juxtaposition, the author builds a life. But once contemplated in full, and in relationship to his other books and accomplishments, a bigger pattern emerges. This is not just a reflection on the life of Bruce Piasecki, businessman and scholar, entrepreneur and family man. Piasecki becomes, in effect, every man here, dramatizing the sorrows and joys that come into our lives, taking us through his experiences, allowing us to enter his world in ways that become our world, as readers. That is a gift that keeps yielding, part Whitmanesque, part Shakespearean, and always Piasecki.

The Art of Being a Dog

In 2014, he gave a reading at the NorthShire bookstore in Manchester, Vermont. It proved clarifying for both his identity and his reputation. It was an alert grouping of people, and he remembered how cold the marble stones were outside the front door, and how warm he became in the act of being himself. It was there that he found a perspective on his writer's life.

He had once known a dog named Zachary. Zach would limp for affection and attention. He might be sniffing the ground, but he was always eyeing something better. Zach was a fantastic dog, warm and fuzzy, smart and tenacious.

Nonetheless, he was easily distracted by a new smell or a new thought; even squirrels could instantly change his calculating equation—and he'd sprint off, forgetting the limp that had gotten him noticed in the first place.

In youth—and even in middle age—there were so many ways in which he felt like Zach, felt himself exactly like a dog. For years, he thought this was because he had come into the world poor, with little advantage except his senses and wit, but now he knew better.

Colette thought that her dad-man had been a bear in another life, "because you protect your cubs, and because you are big and cuddly." Not really, he thought—the deeper, less romantic truth was that he was a dog. No adults really felt him to be a bear, and while he loved his young Artemis daughter, he felt that she exaggerated his size and reach.

His animal spirit was reflective of his deep nature. What was funny was that they, the public, kept feeding him, prompting him. Opponents on the basketball court, whenever he caught them in a fake, called him a dog; early business partners, like Robin, who had owned paintings by Rembrandt, paused when he'd bought them out, to call him a dog. When he met his investors' obligations and left the world of debt before age forty, some had called him un-American—but most had called him, behind his back, "another white Cornell-bred dog." They were usually from the better breed of schools like Harvard, INSEAD, the London School of Economics, or the Manchester School of Business—and their deans and faculty had come from similar pedigrees. He took no offense; but as he did on the basketball court, he chose to make their offense the object of his skill.

Why had it taken him so many decades to accept the obvious? God had granted him a dog's curiosity since his birth in that home near the railroad tracks. Nothing more, little less. Yet it was nothing short of hilarious and gracious and good that the big men and the big women in society kept rewarding him for being dog-like. At church, a minister asked that the social progressives in his community become like boa constrictors—"We need you to be bold, open, and affirmative! Amen! That is our calling in life. Be a boa—offer yourself to a life of action for the good."

Bruce felt that the metaphor of being a good dog was much more convincing. He was afraid to tell his minister this. He knew to go with what interested him, until something even better roamed before him. Having survived a rather turbulent youth, he thought: "You can always go back to the original smells, and find a place to leave your mark."

He began thinking that the good deals that had granted him privilege had resided somewhere in his brain before they became real. This was his most fascinated thought since the birth of his daughter—spunk was in him all along, and it was about learning to let it out. Many spoke of the importance of self-esteem, others about self-worth, and a few more missionaries harped about the certainty of wealth as a sign of divine obligation. This all seemed a bit elevated in his mind, for he knew business to be pedestrian, and success a collection of white scattered bones.

Dante taught him that most lives are more a divine comedy than some stately sequence. His position between the inferno of self-interest and the hells of business and literary accomplishment were punctuated by many adventures in realms of more pleasant, heavenly things, such as the smile of a girl or the chase of a dog in the park. Each peak of pleasure seemed to matter more as he aged, and memories came in the scent of a woman, in the muddy trail of a deal, in running so fast that he sometimes ran right over the petrified squirrels he was chasing.

Memory was stored like the smells in a dog—by intensity, by category, and in a vast and complex system of recall.

After the discovery of Colette, he began to dig deeper, sniffing around a bit, to see what was still out there.

Coastal Bliss Exists

He thanked God for seashells. When feeling generous, he even thanked the Long Island beaches where shells were found—free, adorable, and awaiting his hands. But he came to thank his wife even more.

Since his childhood, he had found great relief in looking through the Golden Nature guide *Seashells of the World*. Years later and far from the sea, he still had that $1.25 edition in his home office. He cherished this small book.

Yet his most amazing find, his shell of shells, was his wife, Varlissima: a woman who contained all women. In the course of his life, he would come to believe there was something special and historic in a composite. Varlissima herself embodied these higher facts. If there was any lasting meaning in the word "supernatural," it had to do with these formations of composites in his life, starting with Varlissima. She was part his mother, part his early lovers, yet completely herself.

Varlissima was at times as dark as the olive shells of Africa; at other times, she was white, with the shape and spin of a tulip shell. For him, watching her eyebrows was blissful, pure joy.

Variety was the essence of Varlissima, a most passionate woman. Shakespeare could write about his dark lady and about his fair youth, but he would write about Varlissima, the woman who knew the oceans would rise years before the warning became real.

Her hand gestures, her raised eyebrows, her change-able smile proved alarming and more worthy than the simple shells of his youth. The heart and soul of Varlissima, this bright vegetarian from Yonkers, was pure energy to this ex-athlete. And the tension in being near her was always tender and alert.

His coaches had said the same thing about basketball, but Varlissima was saying it about their life. This changed his sense of self, and his sense of purpose all at once.

She said the profound in the shape of disarming jokes. "Why were men given larger brains than dogs?" she once asked him at Sapsucker Woods outside the Cornell campus. "So they will not hump a woman's legs during the start of a cocktail party!" "Why does it take one million sperm to fertilize a female egg? Sperm refuse to stop and ask for directions."

For years, he would walk with Varlissima—miles at a time, sometimes a dozen in a day—trying to calm her, hoping for calm in her. He wanted to hear that whisper again, the oceans within her. It often proved difficult.

In his memory, she remained troubled, as if in a storm. This was part of her appeal, something only sex seemed to calm for the few first decades. Varlissima was the rage of Italian oceans, the chill outside each Roman pensione they strove to share.

Thirty years later, she still remembered how cold she had been the night she walked with him and a few friends to Midnight Mass on Christmas Eve in Venice. In her he sensed the inevitability of flooding in San Marco.

She remained a shell of shells, full of variety, full of the charm of surprise, and the force of a storm. Between them remained a space, a difference of immense consequence and certain closeness.

The First Obsession

He received tenure at Rensselaer early in life, in the Management School, running his own Master of Science program. But this did not suffice. Reading was his first obsession. Born to disadvantage, but enabled by the grace of good books, reading was to him as basic as breathing. It seldom left his side.

When Colette was about ten, the family had taken a vacation to Portland, Oregon. There, he sat one afternoon with his daughter on a park bench that had at one end, a statue of a seated man: the man was relaxed, his left ankle resting on his right thigh, and he wore a broad-rimmed hat to protect his face from the sun.

But what stuck in his mind, in finding a photograph from that afternoon, was neither the statue nor the park, nor the pleasure of being with his daughter. What he remembered was that on that bench between him and Colette lay a book.

For years afterward, whenever Colette was away, the image of that book sitting between them would haunt him. Why could he not have sat alone with Colette, in a blinding immediacy?

Half the trouble with this reading obsession came from the ways that good reading came to erase obstacles for him. Reading had reshaped the contours of misfortune in his youth, and then outdistanced his self-doubt upon meeting women like Varlissima. Reading was full of symbolic domination.

The other half of this first and lasting obsession was that it could suspend time. Reading was the only tonic that calmed the speed of time for him. As he sat surrounded by pages, engaged in another's narratives, imagining other lives, suddenly decades would pass, and he would emerge more informed with daughter and wife.

A Maddening Couple

They made a maddening couple to friends, who claimed they embodied opposites. "Opposites attract," his loving biological sister Terry would often say. She was the meat in the shell, and he was the shell. He was the aggressor. She was one of the infinites who absorbed his aggression. She was becoming him, and he was becoming her. He could live with this tension; Mr. and Mrs. Tolstoy had. In fact, he used his sense of couple-hood to hide some personal and spiritual crises, and that felt good. She was the ocean, and he remained coastal in his bliss.

As they walked the long, skeletal coasts of southwest Sicily, they paused, hand in hand, to view the majestic waves, to feel the heat, and to breathe in the salty air. It was only the two of them there—before the discovery of Colette—and it was there that they never resolved their differences, and it was there that they became resolved.

One walks the earth alone or with a keen other. He found his keen other in Varlissima. Yet still she remained troubled, a woman stirred like a top of ceaseless emotion. He could eat a steak. Take a long nap. Awake to find her looking lovely—and exactly like her volatile self, reading, but not calm.

The more she talked, the more her hair made sense to him.

It was large hair, and red. Her soft voice made many youthful narratives in his mind. He wanted, so badly, to capture the essence of that voice to share it whenever he could. Otherwise, he feared it might disperse, like the misty memories of his father. After many decades with this wife, he started to write about their youth, and about his immense longing during their days with their daughter.

Together they began to recall the many missing persons who had visited their home. Writing their recollections was his way of honoring those who were gone.

Unexpectedly, this coupling of fear and joy with her enabled him to become even more appreciative of the valor in women.

The Wind in His Backyard

There were five corners to his property. The Old Stone Church, his home itself, the company offices, and the old barn were peaked by a fifth corner where the prior owner's wife had constructed a small building to sing her operas. These five corners defined the property from which he did his earning, growing, and sharing.

These five corners produced the winds of change that had always stood strong behind him—waving him on, tempting a boy from West Islip to ask the bigger questions—while the Old Stone Church stood solid, defying his tiny ambition with its stone certainty. The uneven rock face reminded him, daily, that it, not he, was proud testimony to the passing of even the strongest winds. It had stood there, quietly, since 1824.

There was something deep and astonishing about wind—something that kept him going, pushing him from behind, something that did not destroy his hope. It said: "*Fervor is more important than fame, zeal more worthy than worth.*" He had never read this in a book, yet he felt this mantra deep as part of his heart, pumping his blood. Wind was worldly, event-based, and more mysterious than formal thought. Where once only women dwelled, the wind now formed a source of his inspiration. Whenever sick, he simply found a way outside and sat with the wind, cup of tea in hand, cigar unlit, and soon felt better.

He saw that his proportionate, ego-based self—the self by which he had been measuring his accomplishments and bankbook—had operated under a recurrent, insistent, functional deception, an illusion of certainty, despite the fact that some things are beyond proportion, like wind.

"What if the things that matter most, in the end, are beyond measure? Is that the best way to define God?" he asked.

Boldly overweight and overworked, he stood as if against a final wall that held him up. He leaned into his next thinking—as one leans into the wind when it blows bitter cold.

But this time the wind was warm, and the lean comfortable. He said, "The computational self, the self that measured what mattered in the everyday, that calculated and assigned value to things, had been a strong force in youth"—but as he aged into this new stance, he began to round things off and to wonder where wind comes from, and why it is usually there, but invisible, subtle, and intractable. There are even winds, he felt now, that only follow rivers.

He loved all this whirling around the Old Stone Church: the simple way the wind spoke to him in the fall and winter—shaking his trees, and at times threatening to bring down the old twisted limbs and trunk of the money tree, but never really bothering to do it.

Life was now all about his backyard; it was all about the wind, about the wind's temporary resistance to the deeper meanings that meant we were alive.

ABOUT THE AUTHOR

This is the 24th book by Bruce Piasecki, since his 1990 bestseller *In Search of Environmental Excellence.* His 2014 *New York Times* bestseller *Doing More with Less: The New Way of Winning* also became listed on bestseller lists at *USA Today*, *Publisher's Weekly*, and the *Wall Street Journal.*

Like his novel *2040: A Fable* and his memoir *Doing More with One Life: A Writer's Journey*, this book is a collection of poetic prose in vignette form.

Bruce was named to *Worth* magazine's Worthy 100 for 2024. This prestigious list honors 100 individuals making the most significant impact on the world, including innovators from diverse fields such as art, entertainment, business, government, nonprofits, and philanthropy.

In 2025, PBS is developing a documentary about Piasecki's career-long work, currently titled "Doing More with Less: The Ben Franklin Way".